"They say this was the way it was . . .
a long time ago . . ."

LIBRARY OF CONGRESS CATALOGING-IN-PUBLICATION DATA
Cohlene, Terri, 1950-
Dancing Drum / by Terri Cohlene; illustrated by Charles Reasoner.
p. cm. — (Native American legends)
Summary: Retells the Cherokee legend in which Dancing Drum tries to make Grandmother Sun smile on The People again. Also describes the history and culture of the Cherokee Indians.
ISBN 0-86593-007-4
I. Cherokee Indians—Legends. 2. Cherokee Indians—Social life and customs—Juvenile literature. [1. Cherokee Indians—Legends. 2. Cherokee Indians—Social life and customs. 3. Indians of North America—Legends. 4. Indians of North America—Social life and customs.] I. Title. II. Series.
E99.C5C675 1990
398.2'089975                          AC          CIP          90-8288

# Dancing Drum

## A CHEROKEE LEGEND

WRITTEN AND ADAPTED BY TERRI COHLENE
ILLUSTRATED BY CHARLES REASONER
DESIGNED BY VIC WARREN

THE ROURKE CORPORATION, INC.
VERO BEACH, FLORIDA 32964

One day long ago, when souls could still return from the Land of the Spirits, the Sun looked down upon the Earth. "The People of the Mountain do not like me," she said to her brother, the Moon. "See how they twist up their faces when they look to the sky."

"Ah, but they love me," replied the Moon. "They smile when they see me, and they make music and dance and send me songs." This did not please the Sun, for she thought she was more important than her brother, and more deserving.

That night, as she always did, the Sun visited her daughter for the evening meal. "How can The People love my brother and not me?" she asked. "I will show them it is unwise to offend me!" And the next morning, followed by the next and the next, she sent scorching heat onto the land.

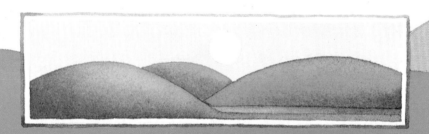

uring this time of the angry Sun, there lived in a small Cherokee village, a boy named Dancing Drum. He saw the suffering of his people. The crops no longer flourished, the children no longer laughed, the old women no longer gossiped, and the river, Long Man, was drying up. Soon, there would be no water even for drinking.

Dancing Drum went to the Shaman, and asked, "Why is Grandmother Sun burning the land and The People? How can we make her stop?"

The Shaman drank the last drop of water from her drinking gourd. "I do not know," she said. "But in a dream, a woodpecker came to me and told me to go to the little men in the wood. Alas, I have grown too weak to travel. You are young and strong. It is up to you to go."

Honored to be chosen for such an important mission, Dancing Drum followed the Shaman's directions and soon found the little men in the wood. "How can we make Grandmother Sun stop burning The People?" he asked them.

"You must go to the Land of the Sky People and kill the Sun before she destroys us all," they said. "First, take these snake rattles and tie them onto your moccasins."

As soon as he did this, Dancing Drum felt a strange tingling flow from his heels to his head. Suddenly, he could not move his arms, and when he tried to move his legs, he only heard the shaking of the rattles. He called for help. "Hsssssss!" was all he could say, for he had become a snake!

"Do not worry," said the leader of the little men. "You will be yourself again when your task is complete." He pointed to a small opening in the underbrush. "Now follow this path to the house of the Sun's daughter. In the morning, when the Sun comes out, bite her quickly."

Soon, Dancing Drum became used to the sidewinding movements of his new body. He slithered along the path into the woods, up the tallest mountain, and through the mist to the clouds themselves. At last, he came upon a large domed house made of mud and cane. It was the house of the Sun's daughter.

Since it was near dawn, Dancing Drum hid behind the clay pots stacked outside the door. I'll catch the Sun as she comes out, he thought. But when the door opened, she rushed by him so quickly, he didn't even have time to strike.

He would have to be more alert next time. He slept throughout the day, and as twilight approached, Dancing Drum was ready. This time, when the Sun drew near, he tensed to spring at her. But at the last instant, he turned away, blinded for a moment by her brilliance.

must try again, he vowed, and this time, I will not miss. Through the night he waited. As soon as he heard stirrings from inside the house, he slithered to the door and closed his eyes.

"Forgive me, Grandmother Sun," he hissed. A moment later, the door opened and Dancing Drum struck. He felt his fangs sink deep into her ankle. But when he looked, he saw that it was not the Sun, but her daughter who lay dead on the ground.

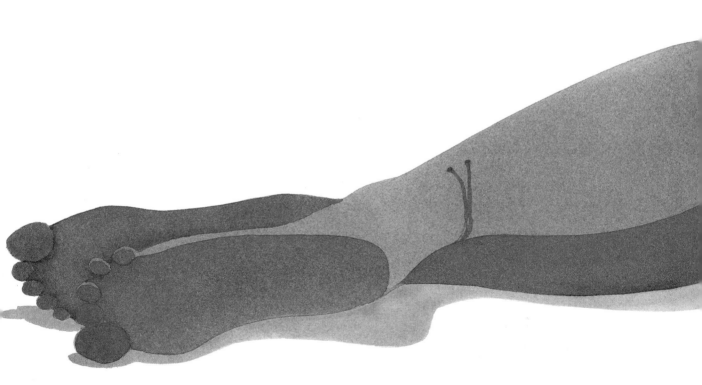

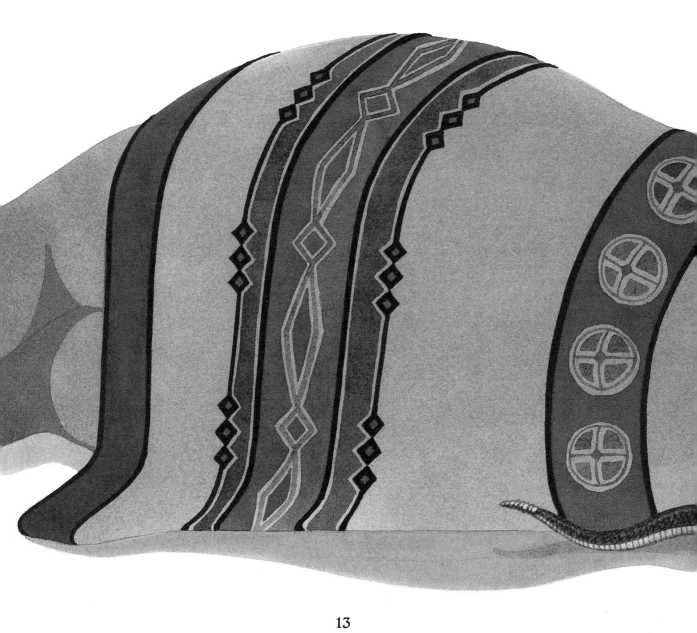

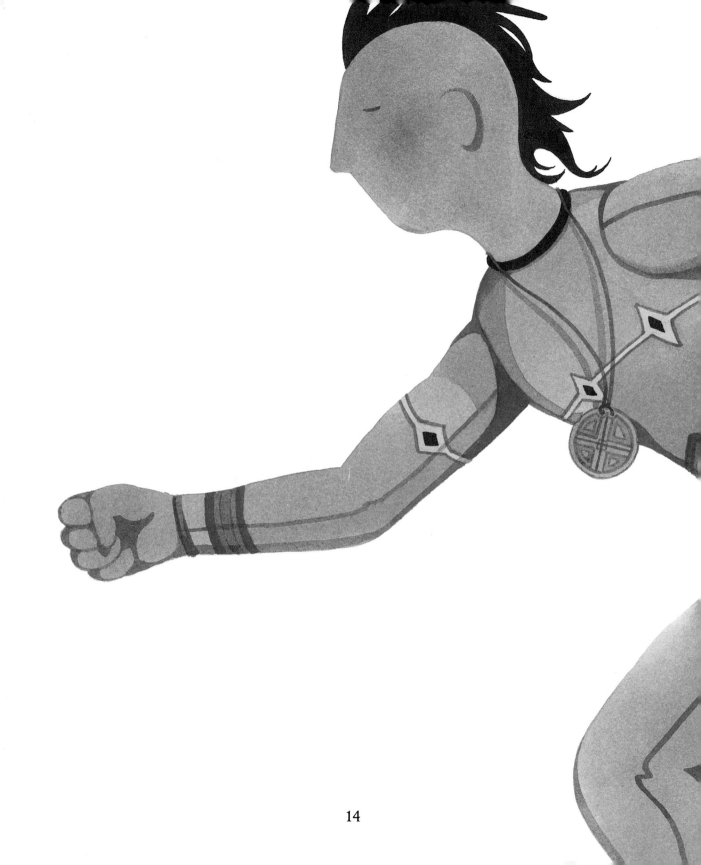

Just then, Dancing Drum shed his scaly skin. He was a boy once more. With the Sun's wail filling the air, he ran from the Land of the Sky People. Over the clouds he went, through the mist, and down the tallest mountain. After many days, he reached his village.

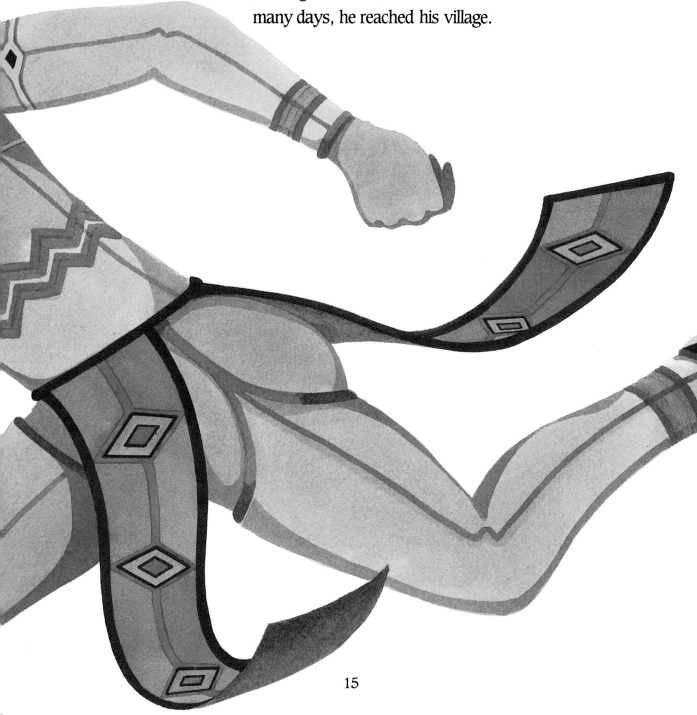

There, the chief was holding counsel. "At last, we have relief from Grandmother Sun's burning heat," he said. "But, in her sadness over the death of her daughter, she no longer leaves her house." He pulled his robe tighter around his shoulders. "Now, The People are cold and in darkness."

Stepping into the chief's circle, Dancing Drum announced, "I am the cause of this darkness. I stopped the heat, but our suffering grows worse. I will go to the Land of the Spirits and bring back the Daughter of the Sun. Then our grandmother will once again smile upon The People."

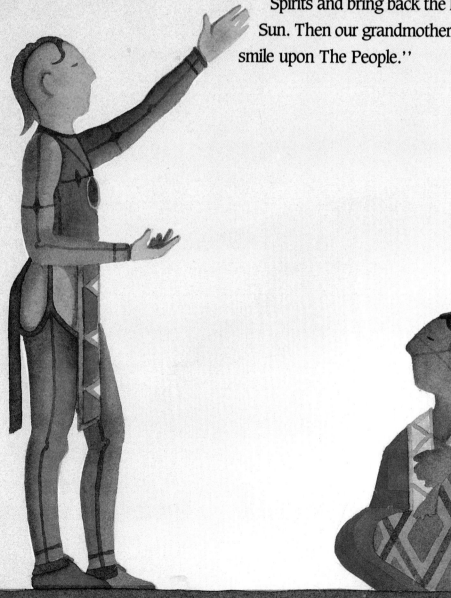

Once more, Dancing Drum consulted the Shaman. "Take six others with you," she advised, "and a large basket. You will find the Daughter of the Sun dancing with the ghosts in Tsusgina'i. Each of you must touch her with a sourwood rod. When she falls to the ground, put her into the basket and secure the lid. Then bring her back here."

"This we shall do," answered Dancing Drum. He chose six of the swiftest stickball players in the village.

They were about to leave for the Darkening-land when the Shaman cautioned, "Once you have her in the basket, do not lift the lid."

For days, the runners followed the path to the
Land of the Spirits. At the end of the seventh day, they
heard drums and chanting, then they saw the ghosts,
circling around a low fire. The Daughter of the Sun
danced in the outer ring, heel-toe, heel-toe.

rom their hiding place in the shrubs, Dancing Drum and his companions took turns reaching out with their sourwood rods. Each time the Daughter of the Sun passed, one of them touched her. Dancing Drum's rod was the seventh. As it brushed her, she collapsed. The ghosts seemed not to notice, so the boys hastily picked her up, put her into their basket, and secured the lid tightly.

After a time, the Daughter of the Sun started moving around in the basket. "Let me out!" she called to the runners. "I must eat!" At first, the seven ignored her. Then she called, "Let me out! I must have water!" Again, her plea went unanswered.

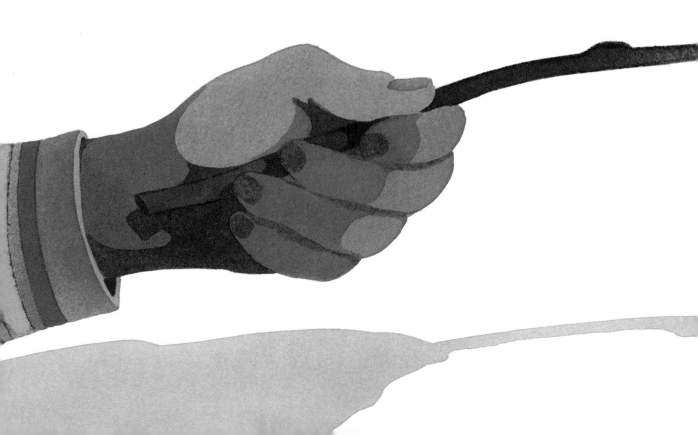

When they were almost to the village, the basket started to shake. "Let me out," called the Daughter of the Sun. This time, her voice sounded strangled. "I cannot breathe!" she croaked. Dancing Drum was afraid she might die again, so he opened the lid a tiny crack.

Suddenly, a flapping sound came from inside the basket, and a flash of red flew past, followed by the "Kwish, kwish, kwish!" cry of a redbird. Not sure what had happened, Dancing Drum quickly refastened the lid and hurried with his companions back to the village.

Once there, the Shaman opened the basket. It was empty! The Daughter of the Sun had been transformed into the redbird. ''You disobeyed,'' the Shaman said to Dancing Drum. ''For this, souls can no longer be returned from the Land of the Spirits.''

Dancing Drum hung his head, and Grandmother Sun, watching from the Sky World, began to weep. She cried so hard, her tears filled Long Man to overflowing, threatening a great flood over the land.

"What shall we do?" The People cried.

"We shall sing!" declared Dancing Drum. So The People put on their most beautiful clothes of embroidered buckskins. They wore necklaces of deer and panther teeth, and painted their faces white. They lifted their faces to the sky and chanted for Grandmother Sun. They drummed, and kept rhythm with their gourd rattles. But still Grandmother Sun grieved.

inally, Dancing Drum left the singing and went to his lodge for his own drum. It had been a special gift from his grandfather. He filled the hollow log with water and dampened the groundhog skin. At last he was ready. Returning to the group of singers, he sat and began playing his own song.

From the Land of the Sky People, Grandmother Sun heard the new music. She stopped crying and looked down to see her beautiful people smiling up at her. She saw them offering their special dances, and she heard their special song.

Dancing Drum lifted his face to the sky as he played from his heart for his ancestors, for his people, and for his land. And as he played, Grandmother Sun came out of her house to once again smile down on her Children of the Mountain.

# THE CHEROKEE

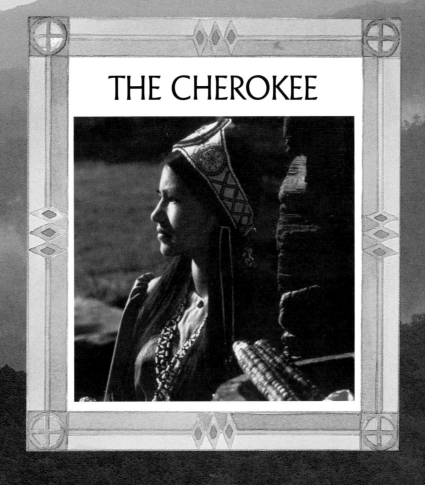

MISSOURI

SHAWNEE

KY.

VA.

POWHATAN

TUSCARORA

N. CAROLINA

YUCHI

TENNESSEE

CHEROKEE

CROATAI

CHICKASAW

CATAWBA

ARKANSAS

S. CAROLINA

CADDO

MISSISSIPPI

ALABAMA

CREEK

KOASATI

CHOCTAW

GEORGIA

NATCHEZ

ALIBAMU

LOUISIANA

ATAKAPA

BILOXI

APALACHEE

CHITIMACHA

TIMUCUA

▷ Cherokee chiefs wore
cloaks of turkey feathers
and headdresses of swan
and white crane feathers
only for special meetings
or occasions.

FLORIDA

SEMINOLE

## CHEROKEE HOMELAND

The ancient homeland of the Cherokee was the mountainous regions of present-day Georgia, Tennessee and North Carolina. The villages were surrounded by palisades, consisting of three rows of upright poles. A large, round Council House occupied the center, and was located near the chief's dwelling.

These were surrounded by the dozen or so domed houses belonging to the rest of the people. Several families occupied each house, which was circular and about 25 feet across. The walls were made of mud and grass, topped by a basket-woven roof. In the winter, mats of cattails, branches, and cornhusks were added to the outside walls for extra protection.

When gold was discovered on their land, the U.S. government forced the Cherokee to give up their property. In the winter of 1838, escorted by armed soldiers, the entire tribe travelled on foot to a reservation set aside for them in Oklahoma.

The journey was called The Trail of Tears. Of the 13,000 who started out, 4,000 people died. A small number who were able to escape or avoid capture hid in the mountains and were later able to purchase land and establish the Eastern Cherokee Band.

## CHEROKEE PEOPLE

They called themselves, "Ani-yun-wiya," meaning "Real People." "Cherokee" comes from the Choctaw word, "Chiluk-ki," which means "mountain people, or cave people."

The Cherokee were farmers. The men worked the soil, while the women and children planted, tended and harvested the crops. Women also wove mats and baskets, cooked, made clothing and pottery, gathered nuts, and cared for the children.

Important occupations for a Cherokee male were ballplayer and warrior. They hunted and made tools and weapons. They were also responsible for building canoes and the house frames and roofs.

Sequoyah is credited with creating the written Cherokee language in 1821. Only a few years later, the first Native American newspaper was published in New Echota, Georgia. ▷

Ball play was an important way for Cherokee men to show their speed and endurance. Each player used two sticks to catch and throw the deerskin ball. Some games had over a hundred players on each side.

The People had a great respect for nature. With the help of their shamans, they looked for guidance from the spirits of the sun, moon and stars, as well as plants, animals and elements. Each year, several festivals were held to celebrate planting and harvesting of the corn. The People made drums and rattles and painted their faces. White, for example, represented happiness.

The Cherokee were known as one of the "Five Civilized Tribes." This is because of their early adaptation to the ways of the European settlers. By 1837, the Cherokee had a written language, credited to a man named Sequoyah, a constitution, newspaper, schools, court and churches. They fought injustices through the U.S. court system, but were stripped of their rights by a president and congress influenced by the settlers' greed.

# ᏣᎳᎩ ᏕᎭᎷᎦᎢᏍᎩ.

## CHEROKEE PHŒNIX.

**VOL. I.**      **NEW ECHOTA, WEDNESDAY JUNE 4, 1828.**      **NO. 15.**

---

EDITED BY ELIAS BOUDINOTT
PRINTED WEEKLY BY
**ISAAC H. HARRIS,**
FOR THE CHEROKEE NATION.

At $2 50 if paid in advance, $3 in six months, or $3 50 if paid at the end of the year.

To subscribers who can read only the Cherokee language the price will be $2,00 in advance, or $2,50 to be paid within the year.

Every subscription will be considered as continued unless subscribers give notice to the contrary before the commencement of a new year.

Any person procuring six subscribers, and becoming responsible for the payment, shall receive a seventh gratis.

Advertisements will be inserted at seventy-five cents per square for the first insertion, and thirty-seven and a half cents for each continuance; longer ones in proportion.

☞All letters addressed to the Editor, post paid, will receive due attention.

ᏣᎳᎩ ᏕᎭᎷᎦᎢᏍᎩ ᎯᎠ ᏗᏕᎷᏥᎦᎢ.
ᎠᏫᎳᏘᎳ ᎢᎠᎻ ᏁᏍᎩ ᏗᏁᏦᎢ ᎥᎿᏂ.

ᏠᎳᎢ ᏗᎾᏩᎵᎠᏱ ᎦᏔ ᏓᏍᏛ ᏩᏥᎵᎠ
ᏅᏓᏂ, ᏔᏨ ᏖᎻᏍᏗ ᏙᏥᎵᏍᏛ.
ᏔᏨ ᏓᏝ ᏔᏫᎡᏗ Ꮦ ᏙᏥᎵᏍᏛ, ᏍᏘ
ᏓᏋ ᎣᏥᎵᎠ ᏓᏍᏛ. ᏗᏯᎡᏍᏖ Ꮦ Ꮽ
ᏙᏥᎵᏍᏛ, ᎣᏯᏔ ᏓᏍᏛ ᏓᏍᏛ.

ᏣᎳᎩ ᎣᏣᎳᎾᎢᏍᎦᏱ, ᏪᏛ ᎠᏯ
ᎣᏥᎵᎠ ᏓᏍᏛ ᏪᏯᏃᏫ, ᏔᏨ ᏖᎻᏍᏗ Ꮩ
ᏍᏛᏍᏛ. ᏔᏝᏘ ᏓᏍᏛ ᏯᏫ ᎤᎯ ᎣᏯᏍᏛᏍᏛ
ᏴᏆ ᏙᏥᎵᏍᏛᏍᏛ.

AGENTS FOR THE CHEROKEE PHŒNIX.

The following persons are authorized to receive subscriptions and payments for the Cherokee Phœnix.

HENRY HILL, Esq. Treasurer of the A. B. C. F. M. Boston, Mass.

of said river opposite to Fort Strother, on said river; all north of said line is the Cherokee lands, all south of said line is the Creek lands.

ARTICLE 2. WE THE COMMISSIONERS, do further agree that all the Creeks that are north of the said line above mentioned shall become subjects to the Cherokee nation.

ARTICLE 3. All Cherokees that are south of the said line shall become subjects of the Creek nation.

ARTICLE 4. If any chief or chiefs of the Cherokees, should fall within the Creek nation, such chief shall be continued as chief of said nation.

ARTICLE 5. If any chief or chiefs of the Creeks, should fall within the Cherokees, that is, north of said line, they shall be continued as chiefs of said nation.

ARTICLE 6. If any chief or chiefs of the Cherokee nation, should commit murder and run into the Creek nation, the Cherokees will make application to the Creeks to have the murderer killed, and when done; the Cherokee nation will give the man who killed the murderer, $200.

ARTICLE 7. If any subject of the Creek nation, should commit murder and run to the Cherokees, the Creeks will make application to the Cherokees to have the murderer killed, and when done the Creek nation will give the man who killed the murderer $200.

ARTICLE 8. If any Cherokees. should come over the line and commit murder or theft on the Creeks, the Creeks will make a demand of the Cherokees for satisfaction.

William Hambly, (Seal)
   his
Big ✕ Warrior, (Seal)
   mark.
WITNESSES.
Major Ridge,
Dan'l. Griffin.
A. M'COY, Clerk N. Com.
JOS. VANN, Cl'k. to the Commissioners.

*Be it remembered,* This day, that I have approved of the treaty of boundary, concluded on by the Cherokees, east of the Mississippi, on the eleventh day of December, 1821, and with the modifications proposed by the committee and council, on the 28th day of March, in the current year. Given under my hand and seal at Fortville, this 16th day of May, 1822.

CHARLES R. HICKS, (Seal)
WITNESS,
LEONARD HICKS.

WHEREAS, The treaty concluded between the Cherokees and Creeks, by commissioners duly authorised by the chiefs of their respective nations, at General Wm. M'Intosh's on the eleventh day of December, (A. D.) one thousand eight hundred and twenty one, establishing the boundary line betwen the two nations, has this day been laid before the members of the national committee, by the head chiefs and members of council of the Cherokee nation, and Saml. Hawkins, Suh.naw. wee, Nime, ho.mot.tee and In.des. le,af,kee, chiefs duly appointed and authorised by the head chiefs of the

mitting murder on the subjects of the other, is approved and adopted; but respecting thefts, it is hereby agreed that the following rule be substituted, and adopted; viz: Should the subjects of either nation go over the line and commit theft, and he, she or they be bpprehended, they shall be tried and dealt with as the laws of that nation direct, but should the person or persons so offending, make their escape and return to his, her or their nation, then, the person or persons so aggrieved, shall make application to the proper authorities of that nation for redress, and justice shall be rendered as far as practicable, agreeably to proof and law, but in no case shall either nation be accountable.

The 10th article is approved and adopted, and all claims for thefts considered closed by the treaty as stipulated in that article.

The 11th article is approved and adopted, and it is agreed further, the contracting nations will extend their respective laws with equal justice towards the citizens of the other in regard to collecting debts due by the individuals of their nation to those of the other.

The 12th article is fully approved and confirmed. We do hereby further agree to allow those individuals who have fell within the limits of the other, twelve months from the date hereof, to determine whether they will remove into their respective nations, or continue and become subjects of that nation; and it is also agreed that in case the citizens of either na-

ᎠᏍᏇᏗᏯᏃ, ᏍᏏ ᎠᏊᏃ ᏣᏱ ᏍᎭᏍᎪᏬ Ꮨ
Ꮥ Ꮙ–ᎦᏐᎠᏗ Ꮨ–ᏍᏔ.
ᎣᎭᏣᎪ ᏓᏍᏇ ᏍᏣᎰᎢ,
Ꮙ ᏦᏣᏦ, ᎠᏘᏥᎦ ᏓᏍᏇ ᎣᎭᏘ.
Ꮟ–ᎵᎢᏯ.
ᎭᏝ ᏓᎷᏍᏇᎦ, Ꮏ–ᏌᎾᎵᎠ, ᏗᏴᎡᎣᏥᎠ,
ᎬᏫ.
R. ᏍᏌᏗ, ᏣᎾᏛᏯ ᏓᏍᏇ ᎣᎭᏘ.
ᏍᏫᏯᎣ, ᏣᎾᏛᏯ ᏓᏍᏇ ᏍᏍᏬᎢ.

TᎡᎢ, 14 Ꭳ–ᎸᎾᏥ, 1825.

ᏏᎳᎠᏯ ᏓᏍᏇ ᎠᎬᏊ–ᎡᎠᏯ ᏗᎨ ᎠᎯᏬᎡᎢ
ᎣᏤᏛ ᎭᏍᏗᎠᎳᏬᎨ– ᎳᎠᏯᎠᏛ, 24 ᏍᏂᎵᎢ
1804 ᎬᎵ ᎡᏍᏥᎡᎵᎢᏍ ᏣᎳᎢ ᎤᎲ ᏔᏍᏏᏇ
ᏗᏐᏣ ᏚᏍᎠᎡᎬ, ᏚᎠᏍ ᎠᏍᏗᏁᏋᏬᏛ ᎤᎾᎵᏇ
ᏪᏫᏆᎵᎠ ᏍᎤᏍᎢᎢᏐᎢ, ᏴᏫᏎ Ꮑ–ᎳᎠᎠᏯ ᎠᏍᏖᎵ
ᎠᏐᏣᎵᏍ ᏖᏍᏍᏇ ᎠᏚᏥᎢ Ꮨ–ᎳᎢᎵ ᎣᏬᎡᎢᏍ
ᎡᎳᎡᏯ, ᎦᎠᏯᏎ Ꭳ.ᎠᏍᏐ–ᎳᎢ Ꮨ–ᎳᎢᎢ ᎣᎭᏍᎢ
Ꭼ–ᎠᏍ ᎠᏘᏍᏬᎡᎢᏘ. ᏚᎠᎢᎬ ᎠᏍᎢ ᏖᏍᎢ
ᎭᏘ ᏍᎦᎠᎵᎢ Ꮨ–ᎳᎢᎢ ᏗᎨ ᎦᎠᎢᎢ ᎠᎾᏥᎡᎢᎲ
Ꭼ–ᎠᏍ Ꭰ.ᏘᏍᏬᎡᎢᏘ. ᏚᎠᎢᎬ ᎠᏍᎢ ᏖᏍᎢ
ᎯᏆᎨ ᎣᏤᏍᎢᎢ ᏍᏍᏬᎢᏗ ᎡᎠᏛ ᎦᎠᎢ– ᎦᎠᏯ
ᎠᏍᏇ ᏍᏫᏯᏍᏂᎵ ᎦᎠᏯ ᎣᏘᏍᎢᏬᎵᏍ.

ᏚᎨ ᎠᏛ ᏏᎳᎠᏯ ᎠᏍᏇ ᏍᏐ.ᎳᎢ Ꮨ–ᎳᎢᎢ Ꮦ
ᏯᏍᎢᏍ, ᎦᎠᏯ ᎠᏍᏇ ᏒᏯᎡᎵᎢ ᏒᎨᏍᎵᎢ ᏘᏍ
ᏒᎵᎢᏍ ᏚᎠᏍᎡᎵ ᏣᏍᎡᏍ ᏚᎠᎵ ᎣᏍᎳᎵᎢ
ᎦᎠᏯ ᏒᏯᎡᎵᎢ ᎯᎵᏯᎢᏐ ᎡᎵᏥ ᎨᎠᎵᏍ
ᏈᎳᏆ ᎣᎭᎬ–ᏏᎠ. ᎦᎠᏯ ᎠᏍᏇ ᏚᏫᎾᎵᎢ
ᏓᏍᏕᎵᏯ ᎢᎯᎵᏯᎢᏍ ᎣᏓᎡᏍ ᏚᏍᎠᎡ ᎣᎭᏍ
ᎳᏍ. ᏚᎨ ᎠᏍᏛᎳᏘᏯ ᏖᎢᎨᎵᎠᎵᏍ ᎦᎠᏯ ᏍᏒ
ᎡᎳᏍ ᎣᏤᏍ ᎠᏍᏯᎡᎵᎢ 1819.

ᏚᏓᎳᏯ,    ᎣᎭ ᏦᏣᏦ.
         Ꮟ–ᎵᎢᏯ.
         Ꮣ–ᎠᏐᏣᎵ,
         ᎬᏫ.
R. ᏍᏌᏗ, ᏓᏍᏇ ᏣᎾᏛᏯ.
ᏍᏫᏯᎣ, ᏣᎾᏛᏯ ᏍᏍᏬᎢ.

TᎡᎢ, 14 Ꭳ–ᎸᎾᏥ, 1825.

ᏍᎳᎠᏯ ᏓᏍᏇ ᎠᎬᏊᏯᏍᏗ ᏗᎨ ᎠᎯᏬᎡᎢᏍ

A young Cherokee woman in traditional deerskin at Oconaluftee Indian Village in North Carolina.

# FOOD AND CLOTHING

Most of the Cherokee's food was provided by their farms. They grew peas, potatoes, cabbage, corn, pumpkins, melons, sunflowers and tobacco. They also relied on wild fruits like grapes, berries, crabapples, persimmons and maple sugar.

They ate fish and game such as buffalo, bear, deer, raccoon, birds and opossum. Like today, favorites were corncakes, corn mush,

Cherokee hunters used blowguns for small game and birds. Here, a length of river cane is reamed out.

parched corn and roast turkey.

Cherokee men and boys wore deerskin breechclouts and moccasins. Women and girls wore short, deerskin skirts. In cold weather, everyone wore rabbit fur capes, or shawls tied over the left shoulder. They decorated their clothing with dyed porcupine quills, and wore jewelry made of bones and teeth.

Woodchuck fur mask.
Many Cherokee masks
were originally used for hunting.

A Cherokee weaver uses plain and dyed split cane to create beautiful patterned baskets.

## CHEROKEES TODAY

Today, the Cherokee are among the largest groups of Native Americans in the United States, and continue to maintain an efficient form of self-government.

Like most Native Americans, some continue to live on established reservations, either in Oklahoma or North Carolina. Many work in oil, tourism, timber, farming or art, while others have joined the non-native populations of cities and towns.

The scroll design of this beaded cloth belt was common in the Southeast.

Known as a burden basket, this large basket was shaped to fit on the carrier's back.

## GLOSSARY

**Ani-yun-wiya:** The Cherokee's name for themselves, meaning "Real People"

**Cede:** To transfer land by treaty

**Cherokee:** From Choctaw, "Chiluk-ki," meaning "mountain, or cave people"

**Choctaw:** Neighbors of the Cherokee, a member of the Five Civilized Tribes

**Gourd:** Vine plant such as melon, squash, or pumpkin

**Palisade:** A fence of stakes built for defense

**Shaman:** The spiritual leader of the clan

**Syllabary:** A type of alphabet using a symbol for each syllable sound

**Tsusgina'i:** The Ghost Country

The Cherokee adapted quickly to European ideas. In 1799, this Cherokee settlement had log cabins instead of thatched houses.

Thatched roof villages were protected by tall palisades. This drawing is based on a painting by Le Moyne, who explored Florida in 1564.

Cherokee clay pots were stamped with designs carved into wooden paddles.

IMPORTANT DATES

| | |
|---|---|
| 1700 | European settlers arrive in Cherokee Country |
| 1776 | U.S. declares independence from Britain |
| 1821 | Sequoyah presents his syllabary |
| 1828 | Newspaper, ''Cherokee Phoenix'' is published |
| 1830 | Andrew Jackson signs Indian Removal Act |
| 1832 | Cherokee win Supreme Court decision over Georgia |

Francis Parsons painted this portrait of Cunne Shote, a Cherokee chief, in 1762.

| | | | |
|---|---|---|---|
| 1835 | Cherokee land ceded to U.S. against majority's wishes | 1924 | Native Americans born in U.S. declared citizens |
| 1838 | Trail of Tears, trek from U.S. South to Oklahoma | 1968 | Indian Civil Rights Act gives Native Americans the right to govern themselves on their reservation |
| 1861-65 | U.S. Civil War | | |

## PHOTO CREDITS

Page 32: Smoky Mountains. Photo courtesy of North Carolina Division of Travel and Tourism.

Page 33: Cherokee Woman, Oconaluftee Indian Village. Courtesy North Carolina Division of Travel and Tourism.

Page 35: Cherokee Chieftain Costume, Oconaluftee Indian Village. Courtesy Cherokee Historical Association.

Page 36: Sequoyah, or George Guess, after McKenney-Hall. Smithsonian Institution, neg. no. BAE 991-a.

Page 37: "Cherokee Phoenix" Front Page. Rare Book Division, New York Public Library.

Page 38: Young Cherokee Woman, Oconaluftee Indian Village. Courtesy North Carolina Division of Travel and Tourism.

Page 39: Cherokee Blowgun Maker, Oconaluftee Indian Village. Courtesy Cherokee Historical Association.

Fur Mask, Cherokee. Denver Art Museum, no. 1936.204.

Page 40: Cherokee Basket Weaver, Oconaluftee Indian Village. Courtesy North Carolina Division of Travel and Tourism.

Page 41: Burden Basket, Cherokee. Philbrook Museum of Art, Tulsa, Oklahoma, cat. no. PAC, C.F., BA 323.

Belt, North Carolina, Cherokee, Early 19th Century. Brooklyn Museum, cat. no. 50.67.24.

Page 42: Cherokee Settlement, 1799, based on observations of Louis Philippe, Duke of Orleans and later King of France. Smithsonian Institution.

Page 43: Palisaded Village in Florida, from an engraving by De Bry, after a painting by Le Moyne. Smithsonian Institution.

Page 44: Clay Bowl, North Carolina, Cherokee, 19th Century. Field Museum of Natural History, Chicago, neg. no. 111430, cat. no. 15514.

Page 45: Cunne Shote, Cherokee, by Francis Parsons. Oil on canvas, 28 x 35 in. London, 1762. Courtesy Thomas Gilcrease Institute of American History and Art, Tulsa, Oklahoma.

Page 47: Cherokee at Oconaluftee Indian Village. Courtesy Cherokee Historical Association.